TRADITIONS IN TRANSITION

Contemporary Basket Weaving
of the Southwestern Indians

By Barbara Mauldin

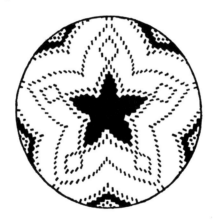

Laboratory of Anthropology,
Museum of New Mexico

■ MUSEUM OF NEW MEXICO PRESS

The publication of this volume and the exhibition which it accompanies have been supported by grants from the Museum of New Mexico Foundation and the National Endowment for the Arts, Folk Arts Program. The travelling exhibition is being circulated by the Education Unit, Museum of New Mexico.

Photographs of basket weavers, 1982-84, by Barbara Mauldin unless otherwise indicated.
Photographs of objects by Southwest Assignments/Vincent Foster.

Designed by Daniel Martinez.

Copyright © 1984 the Museum of New Mexico Press
P.O. Box 2087
Santa Fe, New Mexico 87503

Second Printing, 1987.

Printed in the United States of America.

Library of Congress Cataloging in Publication Data

Mauldin, Barbara, 1949 —
   Traditions in transition.

   Issued on the occasion of an exhibition circulated by the Education Unit, Museum of New Mexico.
   Bibliography: p.
   Includes index.
   1. Indians of North America — Southwest — Basket making — Exhibitions.   I. Museum of New Mexico. Education Unit. II. Title.
E78.S7M33 1984   746.41'2'08997079   84-1071
ISBN 0-89013-150-3

Frontispiece:
San Ildefonso Pueblo Woman Winnowing Grain, ca. 1920.
Museum of New Mexico Collection.

CONTENTS

Hopi Woman Shelling Corn, ca. 1900. Museum of New Mexico Collection.

FOREWORD

The art of basket weaving is nearly 8,000 years old in the Southwest, and it continues to be a lively, active, and productive art among many of the Indians of this region. In ancient as well as modern times baskets have been both simple utilitarian implements and works of art. Particularly in earlier times, they were used for almost every occasion when people wished to hold something, carry burdens, cook food, make music, or present gifts. They were used as sifters, storage bins, water bottles, and wall decorations. They also served as sources of satisfaction and pride for the makers, because it was generally recognized that only the women who were most experienced and who had developed the greatest skill were capable of making baskets with perfect forms, smooth finishes, and complex decoration. Women who could do this were proud of their skills and were called upon frequently to teach their younger relatives and other girls.

Before the Europeans arrived in the Southwest, the early Indians made beautiful baskets with complex, colorful designs. They also developed a number of distinctive techniques for making baskets, or adapted them to their own uses when they were learned from neighbors. The three basic basket-weaving techniques are still practiced to some extent in the Southwest, but the baskets made by coiling are the most common and are among the finest baskets of this type produced in the world. Although some of the ancient forms have been lost, new shapes have been designed for sale to visitors. Most of the bizarre forms which were produced in the early part of the century have disappeared, but Papago owls and human figurines, as well as miniatures, and baskets of horsehair can be recognized as something different from native products in the old style. New designs have appeared in recent years, and contemporary basket weavers continue to experiment with new ideas.

This exhibit is one of the first to demonstrate the fact that basket weaving is still vigorously alive among many of the native peoples of the Southwest. For many years — at least since 1890 — it has been stated categorically, and somewhat sadly, that basket weaving in this area has passed its peak and is rapidly becoming extinct. In some cases the prediction has come true. Barbara Mauldin's diligent research for this exhibition revealed that coiled basket weaving has disappeared among the Mescalero Apache, and it is almost lost among the Western Apache and Pima. The research also demonstrated that coiled basket weaving is being revived with the emergence of some new artisans among the San Carlos Apache and that remnants of the old craft still survive among the Papago, who continue to invent completely new types of baskets.

Some young Papago women are carrying the making of horsehair baskets to new levels of artistry. There are other areas of activity which also make it clear that basketry is far from extinction. The great number of Hopi women making baskets and the high quality of both coiled and plaited wicker baskets are living manifestations of an unbroken tradition. This is also true among the Jicarilla Apache, where an increasing number of women produce excellent coiled baskets as they refine the old techniques and experiment with new colors and designs. While coiling is being re-established among the Western Apache, some of the women have continued to make twined and pitched water bottles. Several have developed twining to new heights with the production of large olla shapes and with excellenty conceived and decorated carrying baskets of many sizes. Both coiling and twining are still being done by the Havasupai and Hualapai women. A conscientious effort is being made by the Hualapai to encourage young weavers by teaching basket weaving in school and utilizing the knowledge of older basket weavers in the preparation of excellent booklets on the subject.

Exciting developments also have been taking place on the northern edge of the Southwest, among the Navajo and the Southern Paiute. The fact that the Paiute have made the well-known "Navajo Wedding Basket" for at least half a century has given rise to many "explanations" for the "disappearance" of basket weaving among the Navajo. In recent years it has been realized — and this exhibit demonstrates — that some Navajo women have continued to produce their own baskets. It has become clear that a great resurgence of basket weaving is taking place among them. Some of their products are in the form of the traditional "Wedding Basket," but new and highly original designs are also being created. The future of Navajo basket weaving will be interesting to watch.

This excellent exhibition will make a substantial contribution to the preservation of the art of basket weaving among the Indians of the Southwest by helping everyone who sees it to appreciate the artistry and skills which the makers have woven into their creations. It will also help the basket weavers themselves to esteem the importance of their endeavors and may encourage more of the young women — and perhaps men — to learn the skills, surmount the effort involved, and enjoy the satisfaction of creating a work of art and perpetuating the traditions of their people. Nothing has been discovered which makes basket weaving much less arduous than it was in earlier times. The modern women who are engaged in the craft derive personal pleasure from their work, however, and the development of a more favorable market for their creations makes the dedication of their time more rewarding than it was a few years ago.

Andrew Hunter Whiteford

ACKNOWLEDGEMENTS

When I began doing research for this exhibition and catalog two years ago, it soon became apparent that the only way to accomplish my task was to go out to the reservations and talk directly with the basket weavers. During the course of my travels I have met many wonderful people who have given me valuable information, advice, and support.

The following people were particularly helpful in introducing me to the basket weavers and sharing information about contemporary basket weaving in their specific areas. Ike Lovato (Jemez State Monument), Terrance Talaswaina (Hopi Cultural Center Museum), Virginia Smith (Oljato Trading Post), Raymond Drolet (Shonto Trading Post), Harry Walters (Ned A. Hatathli Center), Joyce Montgomery (Peridot Trading Post), Edgar Perry (Apache Culture Center), Eileen Gaines (Mescalero Museum), Barbara Groneman (Pueblo Grande Museum), Dennis Kirkland (De-No Music Center, Inc.), Nick Bleser (Tumacacori National Monument), Steve Hirst (Havasupai Tribal Office), Lucille J. Watahomigie (Peach Springs School), and Weldon Johnson (Colorado River Indian Tribes Museum).

I owe a special thanks to the basket weavers and their families, who patiently answered my many questions and allowed me to photograph them. Besides the basket weavers represented in the exhibition and catalog, I would like to mention: Sefora Tosa (Jemez Pueblo), Steven Trujillo (San Juan Pueblo), Edith Longhoma, Griselda Saufkie, Hazil Dukepoo, and Alice and Fred Kabotie (Shungopavi), Grace Harris (Mishongnovi), Frieda Youhoeoma, Rita Talayumptewa, and Mary Jane Batala (Shipaulovi), Eva Hongyawa, Abigail Kursgowa, and Sarah Goshwytewa (Hotevilla), Idella George (Kykotsmovi), Ada Black (Kayenta), Mary Holiday Black, Edward Black, and Maybell Black (Mexican Hat), Atah Chee Yellowhair (Tsaile), Lisa Barlow (Navajo Mountain), Cecelia Henry, Katherine Brown, and Porfilla Porter (San Carlos), Alice Declay (Cedar Creek), Minnie Narcissco (Cibecue), Evelyn Martin, Evelyn Gaines, and Narcissas Gaiton (Mescalero), Avis Dejesus (Dulce), Lyda Thomas, and Charlene Juan (Chuichu), Edith Putesoy, Florence Marshall, Maude Jones, and Bessie Rogers (Supai), Beth Waunueke, Annie Querta, Rachel Parker, and Mammie Machada (Peach Springs), Mary Lou Brown (Parker), and Clo (Glorieta).

I am indebted to Molly Toll, Gail Tierney, and Gail Haggard for their assistance in the classification of the Southwestern plant materials. I am also grateful to several scholars who were willing to share their knowledge of Southwestern Indian basket weaving with me. These are Joyce Herold, Susan McGreevy, Garrick and Roberta Bailey, Florence Ellis, Clara Lee Tanner, and, most of all, Andrew Whiteford.

Lastly, I want to thank my husband Andrew Mauldin, who has been my primary support throughout the project.

Barbara Mauldin

Southern Paiute Basket Weaver, ca. 1871–1875. Photograph by John K. Hiller. Smithsonian Institution Photograph #1610.

OVERVIEW OF SOUTHWESTERN INDIAN BASKET WEAVING

Basket weaving is one of the oldest crafts of the Southwestern Indians. The earliest baskets found in this region, which date from 6,000 to 6,500 B.C., were made by archaic peoples who traveled throughout the Southwest hunting small game and collecting wild berries, seeds, nuts, and other plant foods. Their baskets were simple containers made of sticks, leaves, and grasses which they used to hold the wild plants they gathered and to prepare and store these foods when they returned to camp.

The introduction of cultivated crops into the Southwest after 2,000 B.C. allowed the people to gradually become more sedentary. By A.D. 500, large populations were settling into distinct cultural areas and establishing permanent villages. Their new life-style enabled the groups to devote more time to social and religious practices and to develop their craft arts. During this period, basket-weaving technology improved and more sophisticated forms evolved, such as burden baskets, deep and shallow bowls, trays, and jars.

Since most of these basket containers continued to be made and used by the historic descendants of the ancient peple, we have a clear idea of their specific functions. Burden baskets were used for gathering and transporting food, firewood, ceremonial paraphernalia, and household items. These containers have a large, wide mouth and a deep body, some tapering to a pointed bottom and others tapering only slightly to a flat base. Burden baskets were carried on the bearer's back, with a strap across the forehead or shoulders. The deep and shallow bowls, as well as the flat trays, were used in the home for a variety of utilitarian purposes, including winnowing, parching, washing, cooking, and serving foods. In ceremonial activities, bowls were used as receptacles for sacred materials, turned upside down and used as drums, and given as gifts or payment. Basket jars were used primarily for collecting and storing water. They were generally waterproofed by applying piñon pitch to the interior and exterior surfaces, and were corked at the top with a corncob or a bundle of grass or bark. Worn-out water jugs and unpitched jar forms were also used as storage containers for dried foods, seeds, and flour.

The historic period in the Southwest began with the arrival of the Spanish in 1540. During the next 300 years, the Spanish colonists introduced new types of technology, agricultural crops, and domesticated animals. Most of the native peoples continued to rely on their own crafts to supply themselves with clothing and utensils, however. For the most part, baskets maintained their importance in the domestic and religious lives of the various groups.

The first major step in the decline of basket weaving occurred after the United States took control of the Southwest in 1846 and built railroad lines connecting the territory with the rest of the country. Introduced in the 1880s, this relatively quick form of transportation enabled merchants in the area to import a variety of factory-made goods that could be sold at reasonably low prices. Traditional crafts, which required a good deal of time to produce, were greatly affected. Basket containers were largely replaced with metal pots, pans, and jugs for daily use, although they continued to be important for religious purposes.

The arrival of the railroad in the Southwest had another important effect on traditional crafts. Along with shipments of factory-made goods came curious visitors who were fascinated by the Indian groups and wanted to take some of their handicrafts home as souvenirs. Although many of these tourists were interested only in inexpensive items, others became serious collectors who examined the objects carefully and encouraged excellent craftsmanship and innovations. Many basket weavers responded to the new market and adapted their craft to these demands. During the late 1800s and early 1900s many of the traditional forms were produced in unusually large or small sizes, and some new forms such as hampers, fishing creels, and lidded boxes were introduced.

The economic depression of the 1930s considerably curtailed this commercial market, and many native peoples were forced to discontinue their crafts in favor of wage-earning occupations. In the 1960s, however, a renewed interest in Indian arts and crafts began to develop and increasingly higher prices were paid for good quality work. This trend has continued to the present time, with some fluctuations in the market due to recurring economic recessions. Many Indian artists, particularly potters, textile weavers, kachina-doll carvers, and jewelers, have been able to supplement their other salaries or, in some cases, to give up their outside jobs entirely. Basket weavers have also benefited from this renewed interest, though the evidence of their work has been less visible.

Basket weaving traditionally has been a women's craft in the Southwestern Indian cultures except in the Pueblo groups, where men have also made baskets. These roles continued into the twentieth century, for the most part, with the necessary skills handed down through family lines. When the commercial market declined after 1930, only a few groups, such as the Hopi, continued this teaching process because of social and religious practices. Would-be students in the other cultures had few incentives for learning the complex craft. By the 1960s the basket weavers left in these groups were primarily older women. During the past twenty years, many tribes have sponsored traditional arts-and-crafts programs where basket weaving has been taught. Even in these classes, however, most of the students have been middle-aged or older women who had never learned to weave baskets or had forgotten how. For these women basket weaving is a creative outlet, similar to knitting or quilting, which they can work on quietly at home while they baby-sit with their grandchildren. Despite the renewed economic reasons for making baskets, very few young women in the communities have been willing or able to devote the amount of time required to master the craft. There are exceptions, however, and it is among the active young weavers that some of the most exceptional baskets are being made. Some unusual basket forms are still produced, but the majority of contemporary Southwestern Indian basket weavers prefer traditional shapes. Most groups have a great deal of respect for their cultural heritage; although basket containers are no longer necessary items in their homes, they symbolize the old ways of their people.

The total number of basket weavers found within each Southwestern Indian group today varies greatly. This reflects the size of the populations as well as the degree of religious and/or commercial support for sustaining the craft. In some groups, such as the Hopi and Papago, there are hundreds of productive weavers, while in others, such as the Mescalero Apache, there are only one or two women left. Most basket weavers, particularly those working in the coiling technique, are able to produce only ten to twenty-five baskets a year. Weavers who work in the twining and plaiting techniques may be able to produce more. Many of their finished baskets are given as gifts or sold to other community members to meet religious obligations. The baskets sold to outsiders usually go to local trading posts and tribal craft shops or to collectors who purchase them directly from the maker. Due to the higher level of production among the Hopi and Papago, their baskets can be found in Indian arts-and-crafts shops in cities and tourist spots throughout the Southwest. To acquire baskets from most of the other groups, however, buyers must travel to the reservations.

Unlike other craftspeople, very few basket weavers have been identified as leaders in their field. Collectors may prefer the style of one group's baskets rather than another's, and within this style they seek out the best quality work. Individuals' names are generally not attached to the baskets, however, and shop owners often do not keep records in their files. Reservation traders and tribal arts-and-crafts shops are more conscientious about labeling the baskets they show, but still, buyers are usually not as interested in the name of the weaver as they are in the piece itself. This anonymity is probably due in part to the fact that most Southwestern Indian basket weavers are older women who maintain a conservative attitude that discourages individual prominence or fame. For these craftspeople, the satisfaction lies in producing a good quality basket with a nice shape and a pleasing design. They also feel a sense of pride and a dedication to carrying on one of the oldest crafts of the Southwest.

Navajo Woman Splitting Sumac Branch, ca. 1970. Photograph by Sandra Corrie Newman.
Northland Press, Flagstaff, Arizona.

BASKET-WEAVING MATERIALS

One of the most important aspects of basket weaving is the collection and preparation of materials. As in the past, basket weavers today use plant materials gathered from their surroundings. These range from the young branches of trees and bushes to the leaves, stems, and roots of grasses and other non-woody plants. The choice of weaving materials used by different groups depends largely on the types of plants growing in their specific environments. In some cases, however, weavers may travel hundreds of miles to acquire the materials they want.

The harvesting of basket-weaving materials can be strenuous work, requiring knowledge of the appropriate time of year in which to cut the plants and a careful eye for selecting the best specimens. Once the materials are brought home they are cleaned, stripped of bark, split into smaller pieces, and sometimes dyed. After this preparation is completed the materials may be utilized at once or bound and stored for later use. Before the weaving process begins, the materials are soaked in water or buried in damp earth and kept moist during the work to make them more pliable.

Proboscidea parviflora or *louisiana* (Devil's Claw, Martynia, Unicorn Plant)

Plants Used in Contemporary Southwestern Indian Basket Weaving

    Acacia greggii (Catclaw)
* *Alnus* (Alder)
* *Cercocarpus* (Mountain Mahogany)
    Chilopsis linearis (Desert Willow)
    Crysothamnus nauseosus (Rabbit Brush)
    Hilaria jamesii (Galleta)
    Morus microphylla (Mulberry)
    Nolina microcarpa (Beargrass)
    Parryella filifolia (Dune Broom)
** *Pinus edulis* (Piñon)
    Populas fremontii (Fremont Cottonwood)
    Proboscidea parviflora or *louisiana* (Devil's Claw, Martynia, Unicorn Plant)
    Rhus trilobata (Sumac, Squawberry, Squawbush, Lemonade Berry)
    Salix (Willow)
* *Thelesperma* (Indian Tea)
    Typha angustifolia (Cattail)
    Yucca elata (Thin Leaf Yucca, Soaptree Yucca)
    Yucca baccata (Wide Leaf Yucca, Banana Yucca)

* Used for dyes
** Used for waterproofing

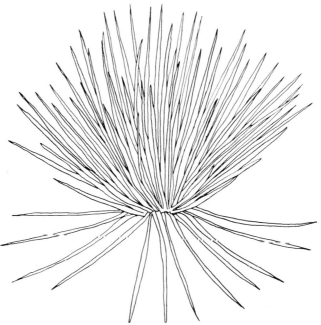

Yucca elata (Thin Leaf Yucca, Soaptree Yucca)

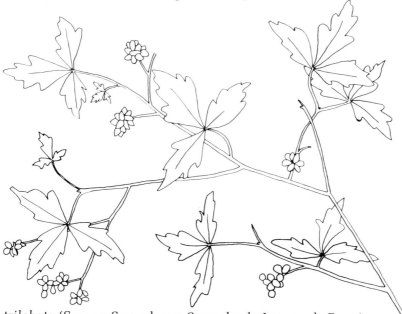

Rhus trilobata (Sumac, Squawberry, Squawbush, Lemonade Berry)

Anita Antone Using Awl, 1983.

BASKET-WEAVING TOOLS

Besides strong hands, good eyesight, and teeth to help in splitting the materials, basket weavers require few tools for their work. Large knives or pruning shears assist in harvesting the plants, and smaller paring or x-acto knives are used to strip, split, and smooth the weaving elements to a desired thickness. Some weavers also use a tin-can lid with holes punched in it to pull the materials through, shaving them down to a uniform size. The awl is the primary tool used in the weaving process. In earlier times awls were made of sharpened bone, but metal awls, often homemade from nails, umbrella spokes, or sharpened screwdrivers, are now preferred.

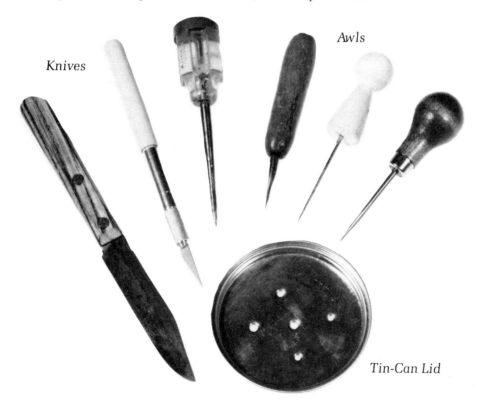

Knives

Awls

Tin-Can Lid

BASKET-WEAVING TECHNIQUES

There are three basic weaving techniques — coiling, twining, and plaiting — which can be used to construct a basket. Although each of these techniques is used in the Southwest, not all Indian groups utilize all three.

COILING

Bundles of grass, wood rods, or other materials are wrapped with narrow ribbons of yucca or wood splints and coiled in a continuous spiral. The end of the coil is attached to the preceding coil by sewing them together with the strands of wrapping. Decorative patterns are created by sewing splint materials of contrasting colors into a desired area on each coil. This has been the predominant technique used since the beginning of basket weaving in the Southwest, and it continues to be practiced in almost all Southwestern Indian cultures today.

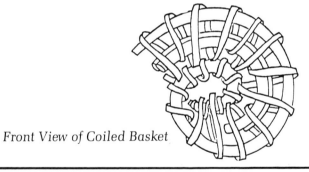

Front View of Coiled Basket

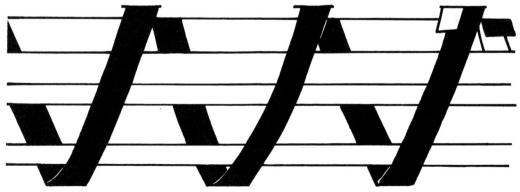

Splicing Colored Splint Materials

TWINING

The twining technique involves twisting two or more horizontal elements, called wefts, around each other as they are woven in and out of more rigid vertical elements, called warps. Decoration of twined baskets can be achieved by varying the pattern of the weave, twisting the weft elements to expose the contrasting color of the bark, or introducing dyed or painted weft elements. Today this technique is used by some of the Apache and Pai groups.

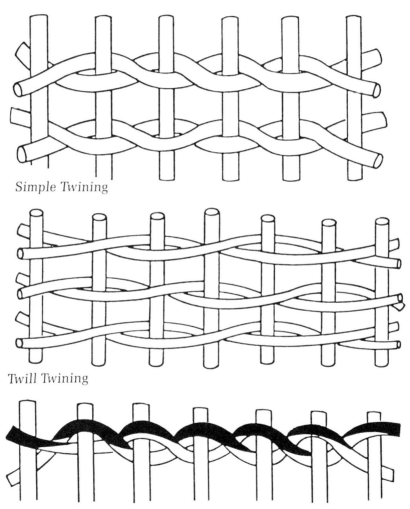

Simple Twining

Twill Twining

Twisted Weft Materials

PLAITING

The plaiting technique makes use of single elements or sets of elements which pass over and under each other in a manner similar to that used in textile weaving. The use of flexible or rigid materials results in different styles of baskets. Patterns are created by alternating the sequence of the weave or by using colored materials. The use of this technique today is confined to some Rio Grande Pueblos and the Hopi.

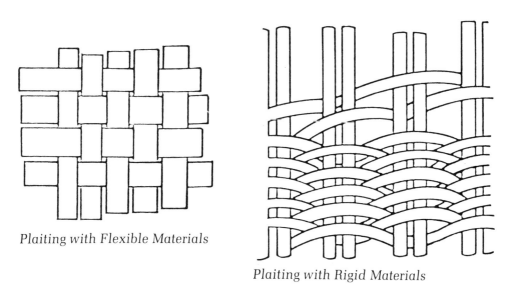

Plaiting with Flexible Materials

Plaiting with Rigid Materials

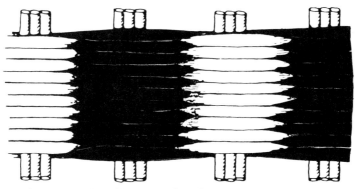

Plaiting with Different Colored Wefts

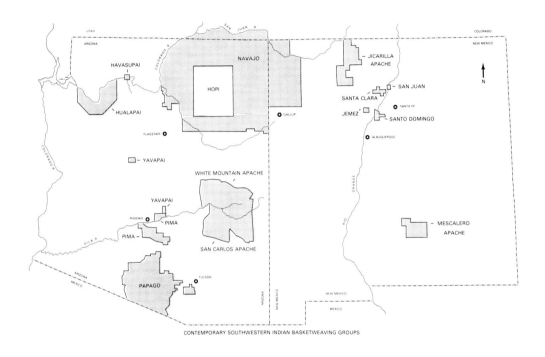

UTAH
ARIZONA
COLORADO
NEW MEXICO

SAN JUAN R

COLORADO R

NAVAJO

HAVASUPAI

HOPI

HUALAPAI

JICARILLA APACHE

SAN JUAN
SANTA CLARA
JEMEZ
SANTO DOMINGO

SANTA FE

GALLUP

FLAGSTAFF

☐ – YAVAPAI

ALBUQUERQUE

WHITE MOUNTAIN APACHE

YAVAPAI

PHOENIX

PIMA

PIMA –

SAN CARLOS APACHE

RIO GRANDE

MESCALERO APACHE

GILA R

ARIZONA
MEXICO

TUCSON

PAPAGO

ARIZONA
NEW MEXICO

NEW MEXICO
MEXICO

N

COLORADO R

CONTEMPORARY SOUTHWESTERN INDIAN BASKETWEAVING GROUPS

Contemporary Southwestern Indian Basket-Weaving Cultures

CONTEMPORARY SOUTHWESTERN INDIAN BASKET-WEAVING GROUPS AND INDIVIDUALS

Although contemporary Southwestern Indian basket weaving can be viewed as a regional craft, many differences exist among the baskets made by the various groups. Most of these differences developed during the prehistoric and early historic periods, when the groups were adapting to their particular environments and establishing their own religious symbolism and aesthetic concepts. One difference can be found in the kinds of plant materials used to construct the baskets, generally reflecting the plants available in the area in which a group lives. Each group also has a preference for certain techniques. Even within the same technique, there are often different solutions to the problems of starting and finishing a basket and splicing in new materials when they are needed. Although the same types of basket forms are made, many variations in shape occur. Perhaps the most obvious difference can be seen in the designs each group uses to decorate its baskets. Some of the motifs are directly related to religious symbolism, but each group also has an aesthetic preference for certain types of patterns and their arrangement within the space. Color is a further consideration. Some groups utilize natural and commercial dyes to create their patterns, while others rely on the colors of the materials themselves to make the designs.

Most basket weavers working today prefer to stay within the traditional styles which distinguish their group's baskets from the others. Within the style, however, individual weavers often experiment with new interpretations of old designs or develop new designs which complement the traditional style. Realistic and pictorial images became very popular in the late 1800s, and, though they are not as frequent today, some weavers are investigating new possibilities. Throughout the history of basket weaving there have also been cross-cultural exchanges in which designs from one group have been incorporated into the style of another. A few of the younger basket weavers today are taking this custom one step further in their efforts to actually duplicate the design styles of other groups. This underlying urge to experiment and express personal creativity has been a primary factor in the evolution of Southwestern Indian basket weaving. It will be interesting to watch the new developments as this ancient craft is carried on into the twenty-first century.

♦ PUEBLO BASKET WEAVING

The prehistoric Pueblo people developed basket weaving to a high degree of sophistication. They produced a variety of coiled basket forms, twined bags, and plaited mats and bowls. By the historic period, however, basket weaving among the Pueblo groups had significantly decreased, and they acquired the majority of their baskets from neighboring tribes. Today, Jemez Pueblo is the only village where a few coiled basket bowls are still made. Although the male weavers who produce them use traditional designs, the bright aniline colors are unlike the subtle blacks and reds found in earlier baskets. There are also several women in Jemez Pueblo who make plaited yucca ring baskets which are used for washing grains. A small number of Pueblo weavers from Santo Domingo, San Juan, Santa Clara, and Jemez make a distinctive type of willow plaited basket which was probably introduced by Spanish colonists in the early 1600s.

26

Jemez Pueblo Coiled Bowl (Wá-shu)
Made by Rosendo Gachupin, 1983
Jemez Pueblo, New Mexico
Ht. 6 in. x diam. 14 in.
Materials: Foundation — Five Sumac Rods;
   Wrapping — Sumac Splints; Colors —
   Commercial Dyes.

My brother and I learned to weave baskets from
our dad when we were young boys. The pattern
is an old Pueblo design used in ceremonies.
I put in the "J" so everyone would know the
basket is from Jemez Pueblo.

27

Jemez Pueblo Plaited Yucca Ring Bowl (Kialas)
Made by Evelyn Vigil, 1983
Jemez Pueblo, New Mexico
Ht. 6½ in. x diam. 19 in.
Materials: Warp — Yucca Leaves; Weft —
Yucca Leaves; Ring — Sumac Rod.

You have to really concentrate to keep the over-
three-under-three pattern right and you have to
go on weaving while you tie it over the ring.
These baskets are very strong. We used to use
them to winnow wheat and to wash wheat, corn,
and other foods.

28

Santo Domingo Pueblo Plaited Willow Bowl
Made by Thomas Garcia, 1983
Santo Domingo Pueblo, New Mexico
Ht. 5½ in. x diam. 16½ in.
Materials: Warp — Willow Rods; Weft —
  Willow Rods (Brown), Willow Rods with
  Bark Removed (White).

I learned to weave these baskets a long time ago
from another Santo Domingo man. I collect the
willows in the fall and strip the bark off some
for the white design. We use these baskets to
serve bread and other foods.

29

HOPI BASKET WEAVING

The Hopi Indians of northern Arizona have a long tradition of basket weaving which continues to play a vital role in their culture today. Baskets are identified with the women's societies and are an important part of the initiation ceremony of young girls. They are also awarded as prizes and given as gifts during other types of ceremonies. There are presently hundreds of basket weavers throughout the Hopi villages. The coiled baskets are produced primarily on Second Mesa and the plaited wicker baskets on Third Mesa. Each of these styles is characterized by bold, colorful designs. The plaited yucca ring bowls and piki trays, which have subtle patterns in the weave, may be made in either area.

30

Hopi Plaited Wicker Plaque (Yuñyá pu)
Made by Marion Kootswatewa, 1983
Hotevilla, Arizona
Ht. 1½ in. x diam. 11½ in.
Materials: Warp — Sumac Twigs; Weft —
Rabbit Brush Stems; Colors — Red
(Indian Tea Dye), Green (Rabbit Brush Bark
Dye), Black (Sunflower Seed Dye), White
(Diluted Latex Paint), Blue (Commercial Dye).

I weave baskets all year round except when I am
busy with the harvest season and ceremonies.
Many of my baskets are made especially for the
weddings. The bride's family gives these to the
groom's family in return for the wedding shawl
and moccasins.

Hopi Coiled Bowl (Potá shibvu)
Made by Joyce Ann Saufkie, 1983
Shungopavi, Arizona
Ht. 6 in. x diam. 11 in.
Materials: Foundation — Galleta Grass Bundle; Wrapping — Yucca Leaf Splints; Colors — Green (Natural Yucca Leaf), White (Bleached Yucca Leaf), Yellow (Yucca Leaf Picked in Winter), Black (Sunflower Seed Dye), Red (Indian Tea Dye).

I started weaving baskets when I was initiated into the woman's society. Now I mostly make the deep baskets with Kachina figures and other designs I like. We pick the yucca leaves in both winter and summer and split them two or three times to make the wrapping splints very thin.

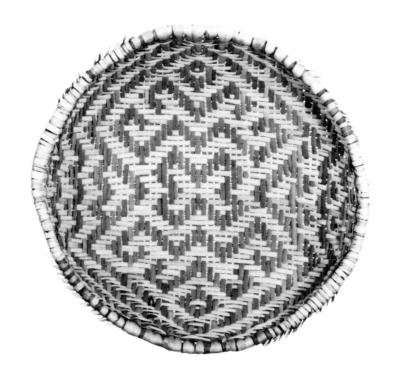

Hopi Plaited Yucca Ring Bowl (Tuchaiya)
Made by Isabel Coochyumptewa, 1983
Mishongnovi, Arizona
Ht. 4½ in. x diam. 16 in.
Materials: Warp — Yucca Leaves; Weft —
Natural Yucca Leaves (Green), Bleached
Yucca Leaves (White); Ring — Willow Rod.

You have to find the longer yucca leaves for the bigger baskets. We bleach some of the leaves in the sun to make them white. A few of the women only do the diamond pattern, but I like to experiment with different designs in the weave.

33

Hopi Plaited Piki Tray (Pikin´ pi)
Made by Fermina Banyacya, 1983
Kykotsmovi, Arizona
Lnth. 19½ in. x wdth. 13 in.
Materials: Warp — Dune Broom Twigs; Weft —
   Dune Broom Twigs (Body), Sumac Splints
   (Edge); Binding — Yucca Leaves.

*I like to take my time with the weaving and do
a good job. You have to keep the materials damp
in wet sand the whole time you are working on
the basket. The tray is used for stacking rows of
piki bread as it comes off the hot stone.*

34

NAVAJO BASKET WEAVING

The Navajo, whose reservation stretches across northern Arizona and New Mexico, probably learned to weave baskets from the Pueblo Indians during late prehistoric times. The primary forms they have made are the bowl and the pitched water jar, both woven in the coiling technique. The number of women producing baskets decreased sharply during the first half of the twentieth century, due in part to the focus on textile weaving. Since Navajo medicine men still needed the basket bowls for ceremonial purposes, their neighbors to the north, the Paiute and Ute, began making Navajo-style baskets for them. In the 1960s Navajo women began to take up the craft again, and today there are over 100 active basket weavers living in the northwestern part of the reservation. Most of these women produce bowls with the traditional red-and-black "wedding basket" pattern, but some of the younger women are experimenting with new designs. The water jar, which is usually covered with piñon pitch, is also made.

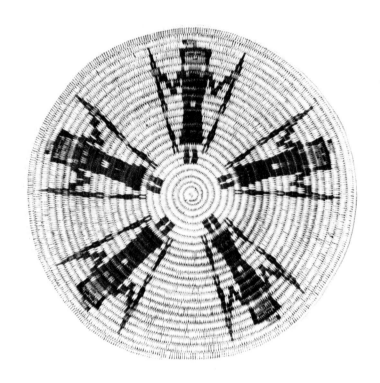

Navajo Coiled Bowl (Ts´aa´)
Made by Sally Black, 1983
Mexican Hat, Utah
Ht. 3 in. x diam. 22½ in.
Materials: Foundation — Three Sumac Rods;
  Wrapping — Sumac Splints; Colors —
  Commercial Dyes.

*I learned to weave baskets from my mother when
I was about fourteen years old. At first I only
made the "wedding basket," but then I started
experimenting with other designs. I use my own
judgement in laying out the patterns as I weave,
but sometimes I sketch them out on paper first.*

Navajo Coiled Bowl (Ts´aa´)
Made by Sandra Black, 1983
Kayenta, Arizona
Ht. 3½ in. x diam. 16 in.
Materials: Foundation — Seven Sumac Rods;
**   Wrapping — Sumac Splints; Colors —**
**   Commercial Dyes.**

We collect the sumac in the fall, and when I run out I can usually buy more from other people. I only make the "wedding basket" pattern which is used by the medicine men. You have to be careful to leave a break in the design so your spirit won't be trapped in the basket.

37

Navajo Coiled Water Jar (Tóshjeeh yishjéé´)
Made by Ruth Adaki, 1983
Navajo Mountain Area, Arizona
Ht. 12½ in. x diam. 11 in.
Materials: Foundation — Sumac Splint Bundle;
Wrapping — Sumac Splints; Coating —
Ground Red Clay, Piñon Pitch; Loops —
Braided Horsehair; Straps — Braided Wool
Yarn; Stopper — Juniper Bark Wrapped in
Cotton Cloth.

The pitched basket jars are used as a water jug for carrying water and also for keeping the water cool and fresh. The strips of horsehair on the sides are used for the handle. A piece of cloth is made to fit as a cover so the water won't spill out. The piñon pitch is put all over the jar so the water will not leak.

APACHE BASKET WEAVING

A number of Apache groups moved into the Southwest during the late prehistoric period and eventually settled in three different geographical areas. The baskets produced within each of these regions have their own distinctive characteristics, some of which reflect influences from neighboring cultures.

The Jicarilla Apache of northern New Mexico traditionally have utilized the coiling technique to make basket bowls and jars as well as a variety of unusual forms for the commercial market. Today many basket weavers work in the tribal arts-and-crafts program, and their baskets are offered for sale through the tribal museum. These women produce baskets with an assortment of bold designs, primarily executed in bright aniline colors. Some weavers are beginning to experiment with a variety of plant dyes which give their baskets a more subtle appearance. Unlike most other Southwestern Indian groups, the Jicarilla Apache only apply piñon pitch to the interior of their water jars.

The Chiricahua and Mescalero Apache, who live on the Mescalero reservation in south central New Mexico, traditionally have made coiled baskets with bold patterns sewn in the natural colors of the yucca leaves. Unfortunately the production of these baskets steadily decreased after the 1940s, and today there are no women making them. There are a few basket weavers in this area, however, still producing twined burden baskets with colorful patterns. Some of these are used in their puberty ceremonies.

The Western Apache area, which includes the White Mountain and San Carlos reservations in east central Arizona, traditionally has been known for its finely coiled baskets with intricate black-and-white designs. Today, there are only a few weavers on the San Carlos reservation who still produce coiled baskets of this style. Twined burden baskets and water jars have also been produced throughout the region and continue to be made by many women on both reservations. Some of the weavers, particularly in San Carlos, are experimenting with new designs and some variations in shape.

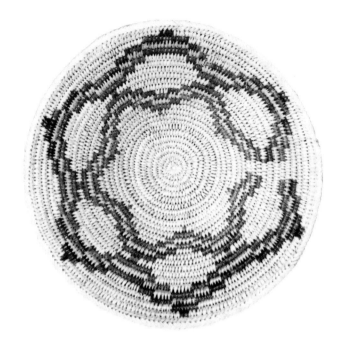

Jicarilla Apache Coiled Bowl (Ips⌒ináska⌒i)
Made by Lydia Pesata, 1983
Dulce, New Mexico
Ht. 3 in. x diam. 14 in.
Materials: Foundation — Three Sumac Rods;
**   Wrapping — Sumac Splints; Colors — Red**
**   (Chokecherry Berry Dye), Light Green**
**   (Bitterroot Dye), Dark Green (Sage Dye).**

*It took me about five years to learn to weave
baskets by watching my husband's grandmother.
That is when I got interested in the plant dyes,
because I wanted something that wasn't so
bright. I like to go out and hike around looking
for new plants to experiment with. Some of the
colors come out better than others.*

Jicarilla Apache Coiled Bowl (Ips∩ináska∩i)
Made by Louise Pesata, 1983
Dulce, New Mexico
Ht. 2 in. x diam. 10 in.
Materials: Foundation — Three Sumac Rods;
** Wrapping — Sumac Splints; Colors —**
** Commercial Dyes.**

I like working for the Jicarilla arts-and-crafts program. We start at 8:00 a.m. in the morning and work all day until 5:00 p.m. We make up our own designs and use the colors we like. We have a belief that the last row on the rim has to be done in one day or something bad will happen to you.

41

Jicarilla Apache Coiled Water Jar (Ko⌢shje⌢)
Made by Ardella Veneno, 1983
Dulce, New Mexico
Ht. 8½ x diam. 8½ in.
Materials: Foundation — Three Sumac Rods;
   Wrapping — Sumac Splints; Loops —
   Braided Horsehair; Ornaments —
   Deerskin Straps.

It seems like I am the only Jicarilla basket weaver making the water jars. It takes me about a month to make a small one. My husband is a horseman, so I get the horsehair for the loops from him.

Chiricahua/Mescalero Apache Twined Burden Basket (Itsiis)
Made by Pauline Kaydahzinne, 1983
Mescalero, New Mexico
Ht. 11 in. x diam. 13 in.
Materials: Warp — Sumac Twigs; Weft — Sumac Splints; Color — Ink; Ornaments — Commercial Deerskin Straps, Tin Cones.

I figured out how to weave the burden basket by looking at my grandmother's baskets. Now I am one of the few people on the reservation who makes these. I use ink to color the materials for the design. The background is the natural color of the sumac or yucca. The tin cones are made from baking powder cans and coffee cans.

43

San Carlos Apache Coiled Bowl (Ts'aa' náskadí)
Made by Mary Porter, 1983
San Carlos, Arizona
Ht. 4 in. x diam. 14 in.
Materials: Foundation — Three Cottonwood
  Rods; Wrapping — Cottonwood Splints
  (White), Devil's Claw Splints (Black).

I collect the cottonwood twigs in the spring and summer when the bark comes off easily. The black devil's claw pods are gathered in the fall. I sell most of my baskets to the trading post and some to other Apache people for the puberty ceremony.

**San Carlos Apache Twined Burden Basket
(Táts' aa')**
Made by Evelyn Henry, 1983
San Carlos, Arizona
Ht. 13 in. x diam. 17½ in.
**Materials: Warp — Cottonwood Twigs; Weft —
Cottonwood Splints (White), Willow Splints
with Bark (Brown); Ornaments — Commercial
Deerskin Straps, Tin Cones.**

Photograph by Mary C. Fredenburgh

*I used to do only beadwork, but I learned to
weave baskets from my mother-in-law. Now I
have a lot of orders for my burden baskets. It
takes me over a month to make a large one. I
just take my time and don't rush it. The deer
motif is my special design.*

White Mountain Apache Twined Water Jar (Tus)
Made by Ramona Beatty, 1983
Cibecue, Arizona
Ht. 12 in. x diam. 9½ in.
Materials: Warp — Sumac Twigs; Weft —
**   Sumac Splints; Coating — Ground Red Clay,**
**   Crushed Cedar Leaves, Piñon Pitch.**

I learned to weave baskets about ten years ago through a program sponsored by the tribe and the University of Arizona. To make the basket jar waterproof, we fill the cracks with ground red clay and crushed cedar leaves and then cover the whole surface with melted piñon pitch. You have to be careful to do it right or the pitch will crack when it dries.

PIMA AND PAPAGO BASKET WEAVING

The Pima and Papago of southern Arizona are kin groups who weave baskets in much the same style. Although yucca plaited containers and mats used to be made in both cultures, today they are no longer produced. Traditional coiled baskets made by these groups have been distinguished by complex black-and-white geometric patterns and some realistic images. There are only a few Pima and Papago women who still weave coiled baskets in the old style, utilizing light brown willow as the background material. Among the hundreds of Papago basket weavers actively working today, however, most have replaced the willow splints with bleached yucca leaves, which give their baskets a much whiter appearance. Many Papago weavers are also producing another style of coiled baskets which features a decorative open stitch, exposing the foundation material underneath. Horsehair has become a popular material among basket weavers on the northern part of the Papago reservation, where miniature baskets are made in a variety of forms. A few of the younger Papago women in this area are producing very fine coiled horsehair baskets with intricate designs.

47

Pima Coiled Bowl (Hua)
Made by Hilda Manuel, 1983
Salt River Reservation, Arizona
Ht. 2 in. x diam. 9½ in.
Materials: Foundation — Split Cattail Bundle;
  Wrapping — Willow Splints (White),
  Devil's Claw Splints (Black).

We pick the willows in March when the leaves are first budding out. I plant the devil's claw in my garden and get two crops a year. The design on my basket is the man-in-the-maze. He was the maker of our people, but he also caused trouble. He built his house in a maze which made it harder for the people to get to him.

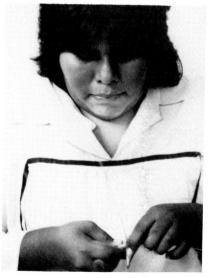

Papago Coiled Bowl (Biṣp hua)
Made by Barbara Havier, 1983
Big Fields, Arizona
Ht. 3½ in. x diam. 14 in.
Materials: Foundation — Bear Grass Bundle;
** Wrapping — Yucca Leaf Splints.**

I am sixteen years old and I have been weaving baskets for a few years. We have to go off the Papago reservation to get our yucca and bear grass, and some years we can't find very many of the good plants. We bleach the yucca leaves in the sun to get the white color. I used different types of open stitches in this basket to make the design.

49

Papago Coiled Bowl (Ha:l hahag hua)
Made by Anita Antone, 1983
Big Fields, Arizona
Ht. 6½ in. x diam. 10 in.
Materials: Foundation — Bear Grass Bundle;
  Wrapping — Yucca Leaf Splints (White),
  Devil's Claw Splints (Black).

Our traditional designs are always started by four. As an old timer I don't count my stitches, I just do it by guesswork. The design on this basket is called the squash blossom. It took me about a month to make, working full-time.

Papago Coiled Miniature Bowl (Kawyu bahi hua)
Made by Norma Antone, 1983
Chuichu, Arizona
Ht. ⅛ in. x diam. 3 in.
Materials: Foundation — Horsehair Bundle;
**   Wrapping — Blond Horsehair (White),**
**   Black Horsehair (Black).**

*I started making designed horsehair baskets
about six years ago. My first baskets were pretty
crude but I worked hard to become one of the
finest weavers. For the past two years I have
developed the friendship design which is now
identified with my work. It reminds me of Papago
rain ceremonies.*

51

YAVAPAI, HAVASUPAI, AND HUALAPAI BASKET WEAVING

The Yavapai, Havasupai, and Hualapai are related peoples who moved into western Arizona from the south sometime during the mid to late prehistoric period. All three groups have produced finely coiled baskets with intricate black-and-white designs similar to some Western Apache examples. Today, there are a few women among each group who carry on this tradition. The twining technique has also been used by the Pai cultures to make a variety of useful container forms. There are many women among the Havasupai and Hualapai who continue to weave in this technique, but it has not been utilized by the Yavapai for many years.

52

Yavapai Coiled Bowl (Ga'u:)
Made by Lillian Shenah, 1983
Fort McDowell, Arizona
Ht. 2 in. x diam. 10 in.
Materials: Foundation — Three Cottonwood
Rods; Wrapping — Cottonwood Splints
(White), Devil's Claw Splints (Black).

I started weaving baskets in my early twenties. No one taught me how, I just remembered from watching my grandmother when I was a young girl. I use both cottonwood and willow, but I prefer the cottonwood because it is whiter. I like to take my time with the baskets and I only make a few a year.

53

Havasupai Coiled Plaque (Gwe buuv lap)
Made by Caroline Putesoy, 1983
Supai, Arizona
Ht 1 in. x diam. 9½ in.
Materials: Foundation — Three Cottonwood
   Rods; Wrapping — Cottonwood Splints
   (White), Devil's Claw Splints (Black).

I collect all of my basket materials right here in the canyon where I live. Since I work at the cafe and take care of my family I only make a few baskets a year. I copy most of my designs from other baskets I see or from pictures in books.

Hualapai Coiled Plaque (Gwe bu:v lap)
Made by Jenny Imus, 1983
Peach Springs, Arizona
Ht. ½ in. x diam. 7½ in.
Materials: Foundation — Three Sumac Rods;
** Wrapping — Sumac Splints (White), Devil's**
** Claw Splints (Black).**

Photograph by Victor Masayesva

I am one of the few Hualapai basket weavers
who makes the coiled baskets. After I collect the
sumac, I split the rods into three pieces and let
them dry. I soak the devil's claw in hot water
and then split each claw into four or more
pieces. I tie these into bundles and store them
until I am ready to weave.

Havasupai Twined Tray (Gwe∓id)
Made by Minnie Marshall, 1983
Supai, Arizona
Ht. 2 in. x diam. 11 in.
Materials: Warp — Cottonwood Twigs; Weft —
**   Willow Splints (White), Devil's Claw**
**   Splints (Black).**

*I made my first basket when I was fifteen, but I
didn't really start producing them in any quan-
tity until I was in my early twenties. I had to
stop making coiled baskets about ten years ago
because I have arthritis in my hands. I still make
the twined baskets and have used some of the
coiled basket designs in my trays.*

56

Hualapai Twined Burden Basket (Gwe gwi: qathaq)
Made by Elnora Mapatis, 1983
Peach Springs, Arizona
Ht. 16 in. x diam. 16 in.
Materials: Warp — Sumac Twigs; Weft — Sumac Splints; Color — Black (Commercial Dye); Ornaments — Dyed Commercial Buckskin Strap and Base Covering.

The plants are getting scarce on my reservation. I have to find someone to take me to other areas to gather materials. Way back the baskets were used by my people for all different purposes. The small burden basket was for collecting seeds and fruits.

CROSS-CULTURAL
BASKET WEAVING

Most contemporary Southwestern Indian basket weavers prefer to work with the traditional techniques and designs which identify their own culture's basket style. Among the younger weavers, however, there are a few who are fascinated by aspects of other groups' baskets. They have begun to incorporate some of these designs and forms into their own pieces. Some of these women are intentionally sharpening their skills to be able to reproduce any North American Indian basket style they choose.

Miniature Baskets Representing Different North American Indian Basket Styles
Made by Tu Moonwalker, 1983
Glorieta, New Mexico

Chemehuevi Coiled Bowl
Ht. ¼ in. x diam. 1¾ in.
Materials: Foundation — One Bullrush Root Rod; Wrapping — Salt Grass Splint; Color — Brown (Walnut Husk and Pecan Shell Dye).

I first learned to weave baskets from my grandmother when I was a young girl living on the White Mountain Apache reservation. Later I worked with basket weavers from other Indian cultures, and today I make miniatures in many different North American Indian styles. Basket weaving is a great teacher for patience and it teachers you to be very harmonious with yourself. Once you start the stitchwork you find yourself doing it in a rhythm.

59

Navajo Coiled Bowl
Ht. ¼ in. x diam. 1⅝ in.
Materials: Foundation — One Bullrush Root
 Rod; Wrapping — Salt Grass Splint;
 Colors — Commercial Dyes.

Chemehuevi Coiled Jar
Ht. ½ in. x diam. ¾ in.
Materials: Foundation — One Bullrush Root
 Rod; Wrapping — Salt Grass Splint;
 Colors — Brown (Walnut Husk and Pecan
 Shell Dye), Pink (Red Geranium Flower
 and Red Petunia Flower Dye).

Western Apache Coiled Bowl
Ht. ¼ in. x diam. 1¾ in.
Materials: Foundation — One Bullrush Root
 Rod; Wrapping — Salt Grass Splint;
 Color — Brown (Walnut Husk and Pecan
 Shell Dye).

Western Apache Twined Burden Basket
Ht. 1 in. x diam. 1-1/6 in.
Materials: Warp — Salt Grass; Weft — Willow
 Splints; Color — Brown (Walnut Husk and
 Pecan Shell Dye).

SELECTED READING

Adovasio, J.M.
  1974 "Prehistoric North American Indian Basketry." *Nevada State Museum Anthropological Papers* No. 16, pp. 100–145.
Adovasio, J.M.
  1977 *Basketry Technology: A Guide to Identification and Analysis.* Aldine Manuals on Archeology.
Basketry, Special Issue
  1975 *Arizona Highways.* Vol. LI No. 7.
Bateman, Paul
  1972 *Culture Change and Revival in Pai Basketry.* M.A. Thesis, Northern Arizona University, Flagstaff.
Cain, H. Thomas
  1962 *Pima Indian Basketry.* Heard Museum of Anthropology and Primitive Art, Phoenix.
DeWald, Terry
  1979 *The Papago Indians and Their Baskets.* Terry DeWald, Tucson.
Ellis, Florence and Mary Walpole
  1959 "Possible Pueblo, Navajo, and Jicarilla Apache Relationships." *El Palacio.* Vol. 66 No. 6, pp. 181–198.
Herold, Joyce
  1979 "Havasupai Basketry: Theme and Variation." *American Indian Art Magazine.* Vol. 4 No. 4, pp. 42–53.
Herold, Joyce
  1984 "Basket Weaver Individualists in the Southwest Today." *American Indian Art Magazine.* Vol. 9 No. 2, pp. 47–53, 63.
Houlihan, Patrick T.
  1976 *Indian Basket Designs of the Greater Southwest.* Utah Museum of Fine Arts, Salt Lake City.
James, George W.
  1903 *Indian Basketry.* Privately printed, Pasadena.
Kissell, Mary Lois
  1916 Basketry of the Papago and Pima. *Anthropological Papers of the American Museum of Natural History.* Vol. 17 Pt. IV.
Mason, Otis T.
  1976 *Aboriginal American Basketry: Studies in a Textile Art Without Machinery.* Peregrine Smith Inc., Santa Barbara and Salt Lake City. (Originally published in *U.S. National Museum Report* 1902.)

Mauldin, Barbara
   1983 "Curator's Choice: Baskets." *El Palacio*. Vol. 89 No. 1, pp. 30–32.
Mauldin, Barbara
   1983 "The Art of Basketweaving." *Southwestern Association on Indian Affairs 1983 Indian Market Program*. Pp. 5–11.
McKee, Barbara, Edwin D. McKee and Joyce Herold
   1975 *Havasupai Baskets and Their Makers: 1930-1940*. Northland Press, Flagstaff.
Morris, E.H. and Robert Burgh
   1941 Anasazi Basketry: Basketmaker II Through Pueblo III. *Carnegie Institute Publication* No. 533.
Mori, Joyce and John
   1972 Modern Hopi Coiled Basketry. *Masterkey*. Vol. 46 No. 4.
Museum of Northern Arizona
   1982 The Basket Weavers: Artisans of the Southwest. *Plateau*. Vol. 53 No. 4.
Newman, Sandra Corrie
   1974 *Indian Basket Weaving*. Northland Press, Flagstaff.
Roberts, Helen H.
   1929 Basketry of the San Carlos Apache. *Anthropological Papers of the American Museum of Natural History*. Vol. 31 Pt. II.
Robinson, A.F.
   1954 *The Basket Weavers of Arizona*. University of New Mexico Press, Albuquerque.
Stewart, Omer C.
   1938 "The Navajo Wedding Basket." *Museum of Northern Arizona Museum Museum Notes*. No. 10, pp. 25–28.
Tanner, Clara Lee
   1976 *Prehistoric Southwestern Craft Arts*. University of Arizona Press, Tucson.
Tanner, Clara Lee
   1982 *Apache Indian Baskets*. University of Arizona Press, Tucson.
Tanner, Clara Lee
   1983 *Indian Baskets of the Southwest*. University of Arizona Press, Tucson.
Tschopik, Harry
   1940 "Navajo Basketry: A Study of Culture Change." *American Anthropologist*. Vol. 42, pp. 444–462.
Williamson, Ten Broeck
   1937 "The Jemez Yucca Ring-Basket." *El Palacio*. Vol. 42 Nos. 7, 8, and 9, pp. 37–39.

INDEX OF BASKET WEAVERS REPRESENTED